CROWN YOURSELF

PILLARS OF LIVING A BETTER LIFE

Part 1:
Personal Empowerment

By Bridget Phifer

Copyright © 2021 Bridget Phifer

All rights reserved. No part of this book may be reproduced or used in any manner without the prior written permission of the copyright owner,
except for the use of brief quotations in a book review.

To request permissions, contact the publisher at
publisher@livingbetterlife.org

Paperback: ISBN 978-1-7377825-0-6
Ebook: ISBN 978-1-7377825-1-3

Library of Congress Control Number: 2021917367

First paperback edition September 2021.

LIVING BETTER LIFE
14311 Reese Blvd. A2-389
Huntersville, NC 28078
Livingbetterlife.org

I dedicate this book to my amazing children, Destini and Christopher, who continually challenge me to be the best I could be. I love you guys. Thank you for being my rock and my "WHY" to never give up and never quit.

To my mom, who has been my ultimate example of a modern-day superwoman. You continually prove that there is nothing impossible.

Lastly to my husband, he never saw a day that wasn't "Phenomenal." You are truly missed and definitely will never be forgotten.

Table of Continents

PREFACE   **7**

INTRODUCTION   **17**

PILLAR 1 – BE AUTHENTIC   **24**

PILLAR 2 – SELF AWARENESS   **28**

PILLAR 3 – SELF ACCEPTANCE   **47**

PILLAR 4 – RIGHT MINDSET   **63**

PILLAR 5 – GOOD HABITS   **77**

PILLAR 6 – GRATITUDE   **90**

CONCLUSION   **104**

REFERENCES   **115**

CROWN YOURSELF

PREFACE

I am going to say something that may sound like I am contradicting myself. I am a Christian. I love God with ALL MY HEART, and I believe his Word. However, I also think that some "religious rules" (Christian and non-Christian) have caused many people to be confused. I think it may be selfishness and misinterpretation of God's Word. I believe that God hates violence and that our relationships should be driven by selflessness, grace, and love. However, it is really sad some use their religious rules and practices to justify wife-beating and shaming. Some even believe that marital success is predicated on a woman being subservient or even slavish. Unfortunately, this is often the basis on which women have been judged or praised.

My Own Experience.

I remember one day I layed prostrate in the middle of my living room floor, and I CRIED AND CRIED. My first husband was abusive. I literally cried on my honeymoon night. That night, I knew I had made a mistake. It seemed he changed almost immediately. I remember saying to myself, "This wasn't what I signed up for." I thought If I do what I was taught in church, surely things would get better. They didn't get better.

Instead, I found myself in a strange new place with no family and no friends. Anyone from my hometown would have been shocked to learn that I was in an abusive relationship. My ex-husband would often apologize and make promises to never do it again. There were times I piled on make-up to cover black eyes and bite marks as I sat in class at the Bible college we were attending. For months I said nothing because I thought it was my duty to cover my husband. I thought about leaving my marriage many times. One time, I packed a few things and went to stay with a couple we met when we first moved to town. I was shocked when they called my ex-husband and advised me to go back home.

As I reflect on that time in my life, the person I had become was not "ME." I can't even tell you how I had gotten to that place. I guess you can say I was so BROKEN I had lost me. I had lost my voice and my vision. Before my first marriage, I was known for my strength. Not only was I known for my physical strength, but I was also known for my strength of mind and character. I was a beast on the basketball court in college, and I worked hard as a black female engineer in a good ole boys world. I had to defy multiple challenges to stand in the room and be heard amongst these men. I WAS STRONG.

What happened to me? How did I find myself in this situation? Maybe it was the scriptures that were often used out of context that caused me to feel powerless. I didn't feel STRONG anymore. I was SO OVERWHELMED WITH MY LIFE. At the time, I believed that God wanted me to stay with my ex-husband even through the abuse and the pain I was in. I blamed myself. I felt like I didn't measure up. I felt helpless and so embarrassed. I wouldn't tell anyone back home what was going on with me. Not even my mom or my best friend knew what I was going through.

I felt like giving up. I should have left, but I stayed. I stayed because I carried around a warped religious belief that I could not get a divorce. I thought that certain scriptures forbid me from getting a divorce. I thought, if I got a divorce, everything I wanted in life would be unattainable and that I would be damaged goods. There were three things I wanted from the time I was 6 years old. I wanted to be a Minister, to get married, and to be a Millionaire. I put up with an abusive marriage because I thought I HAD TO.

It wasn't until I was in the hospital stressed out, preeclamptic, and about to have my baby premature when I realized how disillusioned I had become. I guess you can say I had a Simba moment. Like in the Lion King when Simba met Rafiki.

I spent almost 2 and a half months in the hospital on bed rest. While I was there, I remembered who I was. I remembered what I had inside. I realized I was better than what I had become. I had allowed my situation to dictate to me who I was. Although it took me a while to get there, I realized that failure did not make me a failure. My marriage was failing; however, I was not a failure. I didn't have to give up on my dreams, nor did I have to live a life of misery. Failure was not the end. It was only the beginning. I picked up my crown and reclaimed my throne.

In the Lion King, Simba could have stayed in a place running from his past, ignoring his responsibility and potentially impacting others. Simba chose to take his rightful place as King. Likewise, it is up to you who you become. Daily we choose what we believe, what we see, and what we'll do. Everything in life is a choice. Each choice brings with its consequences, some good and some bad. Our decisions make us.

I decided to return to my pride land and take my rightful place on the throne of my life. I was on a new journey to be the best me that I could be. I chose to leave a life of abuse and was divorced from my first husband. I remarried and had two amazing children. I have also been in Real Estate for over 20 years.

I am a business consultant, empowerment coach, motivational speaker, and a licensed minister. I absolutely love all the lives I've been able to touch. EVERY BUSINESS I've had has been my ministry. I made myself available to help people using whatever talent I had inside. I am now the CEO of Living Better Life, LLC. Over the years, I have helped many individuals, whether with personal empowerment, financial stability, buying or selling a home, or helping their spiritual growth. I've dedicated my life to furthering the success and stability of minorities and women everywhere.

When you go through an abusive situation, suffer a loss, or need to navigate a complex circumstance, you are shaken. My abusive marriage shook me to my very core. I went through every stage of grief on my journey back to my true self. At first, I was in denial about my situation, then I was numb to it. There were times I even needed help to get out of bed. I chose to embark on a process of healing and to overcome my broken and defeated spirit. I did not stay stuck in that place. I decided to remember who I was and begin a new healing journey and be my best self.

When I put the past behind me, I was able to face my true self. I had to examine my thoughts to find the limiting beliefs that were holding me back. I opened my mind to accept new beliefs and changed my viewpoint. I had to change my belief. I heard someone say, "if you don't believe, you can never become."

I thank God as I opened and finally shared my story; my voice was heard. I was able to unlearn some things that were taught and reprogram my mind with good things and good news. I was destined for greatness. I crowned myself and walked into my Queendom.

Knowing and understanding your worth is the first step to Crowning Yourself and walking into your Queendom.

Not every woman's journey is the same. We must decide what we will do with what's placed in front of us and within us on our journey. Crown yourself is to help every woman on their journey towards royalty. My desire is that as you read this book, you will be inspired to become the Queen you were created to be and begin living the life you truly deserve. We all need to overcome the challenges and obstacles we face in our lives. Crown Yourself is designed to help you grow through your challenges, mature you to be the best person YOU CAN BE so that you can start doing the things PURPOSED in your heart, Live to your fullest potential, create a legacy, and HAVE more to give back and help others do the same.

Crown Yourself is a guide to living your best life. It is a declaration to women everywhere that you have a purpose and are destined for greatness. It is a call to your inner greatness to rise and take your rightful place as Queen. You were fearfully and wonderfully made, and you are the healing the world needs.

This book is your blueprint to help you rise above your circumstances and move forward courageously into living life in full. The book is broken into what we will call pillars. A pillar is a tall solid structure, which is usually used to support part of a building. These pillars will serve as our foundation for living a better life. This book is Part 1 of a 4 Part Series. Part 1 deals with personal empowerment. People who are empowered are more in control of their environment, emotional state, beliefs, and ultimately their actions. Crown Yourself begins with helping you show up as your authentic self and be aware of your power and purpose. Accepting who you are and what you have inside is the first step on this journey to be your best self. Crown Yourself will help you overcome limiting beliefs and roadblocks that have held you back. It will help you build habits to help create success in every area of your life. And lastly, this book will guide you onto having an attitude of gratitude and begin to move with unstoppable confidence.

As you become the best version of yourself and tap into your talents, learn to utilize your gifts, and gain monetary wealth. Part 2 of Crown Yourself deals with financial empowerment; it will be released later this year. It explores various fundamentals to building wealth as well as creating a legacy. Part 3 deals with Getting Healthy will also be released later this year. It provides ways to improve your physical health and ways to maximize your spiritual and mental health.

As you move forward on your journey to Crown Yourself and reign as the Queen you indeed are, you will surely start to experience more triumph and victory in your life. On the way, you'll learn many things about yourself and how you can find the courage to proudly show the world the real you. Your journey ends in an exciting vision of a future that you design yourself based on your goals, dreams, and passions. You write your own story. With each of your experiences, you grow, and you learn. You gain the strength and wisdom needed to not only face the obstacles in front of you but to help others overcome them too. That leads us to Pillar 4 - Giving Back, also coming soon, focuses on helping others. Giving back and supporting the people and community around you will make your life and the life of those around you better!

Queen, get ready to start your journey to living a better life and ruling your Queendom.

INTRODUCTION

A TALE OF TWO QUEENS

Have you ever read the story of Queen Esther? The Book of Esther in the Bible tells the story of the Jewish Queen Esther. I have read that story many times in my life; however, when I needed internal healing the most, I came across a devotional that helped me see something I had not seen before. I'd like to briefly share this excerpt from Esther Chapter one from the Message Bible.

Esther Chapter 1 (The Message Bible) reads:

The story happened in the time of Xerxes, the Xerxes who ruled from India to Ethiopia—127 provinces in all...He put on an exhibit for six months to show off his wealth and the stunning beauty of his royal splendors. After the exhibit, he threw a weeklong party for everyone living in Susa. The guests could drink as much as they liked. Queen Vashti was throwing a separate party for women inside the royal palace. On the seventh day of the party, while high on the wine, the king ordered his servants to bring him Queen Vashti wearing her royal crown. He wanted to show off her beauty to the guests and officials. She was extremely good-looking. Queen Vashti refused to come; she refused the summons of a drunken king. The king lost his temper. Seething with anger over her insolence, and called in his counselors, all experts in legal matters. He asked them what legal recourse they had against Queen Vashti for not obeying the King.

The King was told that it was not only the king that Queen Vashti insulted. They told him she insulted all the leaders and people alike in every one of King Xerxes' provinces. They said the word would get out: 'Did you hear the latest about Queen Vashti? King Xerxes ordered her to be brought before him, and she wouldn't do it!' When the women hear it, they'll start treating their husbands with contempt. The day the wives of the Persian and Mede officials get wind of the queen's insolence, they'll be out of control. Is that what we want, a country of angry women who don't know their place? So, the king agreed to permanently banish Queen Vashti from King Xerxes' presence. When the king's ruling became public knowledge throughout the kingdom, it was designed that every woman would show proper respect to her husband regardless of her social position. The king sent bulletins to every part of his kingdom, to each province in its own script, to each people in their own language: "Every man is master of his own house; whatever he says, goes."i

For years I was taught that Queen Vashti was a bad representation of a woman because she "disobeyed" her husband. I was shocked to read a commentary that explained that when Queen Vashti was told to come wearing her crown, it was meant for her to come wearing only her crown, to appear before the king and his guest naked. This type of showing off was for concubines or prostitutes – not for women of honor and certainly not for a queen.

I was taught that Vashti disrespected her husband and "deserved" to be punished. Biblical references like this have been used to tell women to endure domestic violence in the name of God.

Vashti made a choice to not go to the king when she was summoned. Vashti knew who she was. She refused to do something that she felt would disgrace her. She crowned herself and walked in her Queendom as a true representation of a woman loving herself.

CROWN YOURSELF

A Queen on her throne is a woman who has mastered herself.
She's not perfect, but she is complete.
She has come to the full realization that everything she needs to fulfill her mission can be found within.
She has uncovered her powers and knows how to use them.
She is no longer on The Path; she has become The Path.
–Molesey Crawford

As a young girl in church, Esther was one of my favorite stories in the Bible. Back then, I saw a story of a little girl who became the winner of a beauty pageant and crowned Queen. However, when I read Esther now, I see women navigating an archaic period that very much resembles the #MeToo movement of our modern-day male-dominated world. For those that don't know the story, after Queen Vashti was banished from the king, he had young girls brought to him to be judged to be a part of his harem, to either be Queen or his concubine. Esther was chosen to be Queen.

I don't understand everything going on in the story of Esther; however, I believe we can learn extraordinary lessons from these two women. Queen Vashti chose to stand up for herself when women were not expected to speak up for themselves.

She stood on her values and her position as Queen and refused to be treated less than. She spoke up for herself. Yay, Queen Vashti.

Queen Esther was a young girl that lost her parents at a young age. She was taken in and raised by her cousin Mordecai. Esther was an unlikely hero. She starts out as a passive little girl being told what to do. However, we see her transform into a young woman who learns to use her voice. In the beginning, she hid her heritage. Later we witness her courage and wisdom as she outsmarts a man trying to destroy her and her people.

It wasn't until I was an adult that I realized what Esther really went through. It wasn't just a beauty pageant. It was a sexual audition. Each girl, a virgin, spent 12 months preparing for their night with the king. For me, that would have been extremely degrading; however, because of the time period, I guess this was an honor these women may have felt. Each girl could take something with them to spend the night with the king. The girls that weren't chosen to be Queen would be added to the king's Harem. Whatever the girls took with them to meet the King, they were allowed to keep for themselves. I guess that was a type of payment because the girls were unable to marry any others. Esther, however, took nothing. It is like she had a type of confidence, where she knew she was enough.

Esther was an orphan, a minority, a woman who came from humble beginnings. But she was much more than those labels. She became an advocate for her people and helped save an entire generation. During her time, by law, if the king found you in his presence without being summoned, it could mean a death sentence. When Esther found that there was a plot to kill her people, Esther refused to remain silent. She realized that perhaps she had this royal position for such a time as this. She grabbed her Crown and walked into her Queendom, and she said these stirring words: I will go to the king, even though it is against the law. And if I perish, I perish.' **When social rules and laws could mean death, Esther found her voice to save a nation.ii**

"Breaking our silence is powerful. Whether it comes as a whisper or a squeak at first, allow that sense of spaciousness, of opening, allow yourself to trust the bottomlessness, and lean into the dark roar which will light up every cell.

Though it may start softly, we build in confidence and skills, we realize we do not need to wait for permission before we open our mouths. We do not need to wait for others to make space for us; we can take it. We do not need to read from others' scripts or style ourselves in weak comparison. We do not need to look to another's authority because we have our own. Down in our cores. We have waited so long for permission to know that it was our time, our turn on stage. That time is now. Our voices are being heard into being. They are needed."

— ***Lucy H. Pearce, Burning Woman***

Like Queen Esther, your voice is needed. You are needed. The world needs you. Your individuality makes the world a better place. You need to be yourself; you need you. Life can't be satisfying pretending to be someone else or less than you really are. Understand that so many people are trying to fit in because it isn't comfortable to stand out. Overcome the need to be anonymous. Let the world see YOU! Be willing to put your best and unique gifts into the world and find your voice. People are respected for daring to be themselves. Understand that people appreciate you more if you can be comfortable being yourself. There's a lot to be gained by being your authentic self.

PILLAR 1 – BE AUTHENTIC

CROWN YOURSELF BY FINDING YOUR VOICE AND BEING YOUR AUTHENTIC SELF

Find Your Voice and Allow Your Individuality to Shine

Queen, it's not easy to stand out and reveal yourself to the world. We learn early in life that it's sometimes easier to blend in. Just think about when you were in school. Standing out sometimes resulted in being bullied or teased. Even as an adult, society expects you to act or be a particular way. Sometimes it can put you in a box, and you feel you must wear a mask to exist.

> *"To be yourself in a world that is constantly trying to make you something else is the greatest accomplishment."*
> *~ Ralph Waldo Emerson*

You can live the life you always wanted by showing the world the real "you" and catering to what's most important to you. More important than being honest with the world is being honest with yourself. There are so many advantages to being authentic. One advantage is that you'll no longer need to change your words and actions to impress others. You can relax and be you.

For you to be authentic, you must first know yourself. Sometimes you can wear a mask for so long that you lose track of who you are. This includes knowing your values and goals. Authenticity becomes possible only when you know what's important to you. As you read this book, you will go on a journey to becoming your authentic self. On the way, you'll discover many things about yourself and how you can find the courage to proudly show the world the real you.

CROWN YOURSELF AND PRESENT YOURSELF HONESTLY

Give up the need to appear perfect. Your excellence is good enough. Do everything with the spirit of excellence, which means do your best! You don't need to be perfect; just be honest. No one is perfect anyway. There is no need to put on a show for the rest of the world. You can be you and be the true star you already are. Realize the real you is spectacular. Be the best at being yourself. Know your values and live by them. Consistently living by your values will keep you on the road to living your most authentic life.

Have you ever noticed a time when you weren't yourself? You might have found yourself acting differently based on the situation or people you were around. It is better to be your true authentic self than to pretend to be someone you're not. Examine the times you found it challenging to be true to yourself. Do you know why you felt that way?

There is no need to be anyone other than you. Even when it comes to dealing with your weaknesses. Overcoming your weakness starts with you being true to yourself. You should be able to share your opinions honestly and freely. Life becomes easier when you're living authentically. I find it exhausting to constantly change my thoughts, attitudes, and personality to please others. There was a time when I was so concerned about what others would think or say about my actions. A scripture that says not to be afraid of their faces has encouraged me not to be mindful of what others will say. As you Crown Yourself with authenticity, you'll no longer feel the need to protect yourself from others. By investing time in yourself, you learn to be free. You can be authentic with your thoughts, your words, and your actions.

Do you know the real you? You can ask yourself a few questions to help you uncover your true self and start the process of unraveling the real you.

What are some of your innermost feelings and thoughts about who you really are? When are you the happiest? What makes you happy? Are you satisfied now? Do you feel joy in your life? Or do you feel like you're putting on a show trying to keep up with the others?

Be honest with yourself. Think about what you really want out of life. This will help you discover what is important to you. Focus on what you genuinely want and start moving in that direction. Having an honest talk with yourself will help you understand your true feelings and help you stay on track to have the life you genuinely desire. It is an exciting journey to revealing the real you, and it will also fill you with great joy and satisfaction.

"In every woman, there is a Queen. Speak to the Queen, and the Queen will answer."
~*Norwegian Proverb*

PILLAR 2 – SELF AWARENESS

CROWN YOURSELF WITH SELF-AWARENESS

Queen, it's impossible to live authentically without first discovering who you are. Self-awareness is crucial! Self-awareness is one of the essential aspects of personal development.

As you become more aware of the layers that construct the real you, you will discover more beautiful things about yourself. As you become more self-aware, you can change deep down beliefs that have held you back. The journey of self-discovery is a never-ending and eye-opening adventure.

When you become self-aware, you take 100% responsibility for yourself. That includes your strengths, weaknesses, and personality. You even start to become more aware of your thoughts and begin to watch them objectively as an observer.

"To have greater self-awareness or understanding means to have a better grasp of reality."
*- **Dalai Lama***

DISCOVER YOUR TRUE SELF

Dig deep until you can see who you are. The journey starts with the first step, understanding "Who am I?"

The Disney movie, Mulan, is one of my favorite movies. For years I cried every time Mulan sang, "Reflection." I still get a little teary-eyed. My children caught me on video one year crying as I sang the song. It was funny to them; however, my heart hurt because I felt I could not be me, and I was still hiding my authentic self from the world and my children. The lyrics of the song had me all choked up.

Mulan (Reflection Lyrics)
Look at me; you may think you see who I really am,
but you'll never know me
Every day it's as if I play a part
Now I see if I wear a mask, I can fool the world,
but I cannot fool my heart
Who is that girl I see staring straight back at me?
When will my reflection show Who I am inside?

*I am now in a world where I have to hide my heart and what
I believe in
But somehow, I will show the world what's inside my heart
and be loved for who I am*

*Who is that girl I see staring straight back at me?
Why is my reflection someone I don't know?*

*Must I pretend that I'm someone else for all time?
When will my reflection show Who I am inside?*

*There's a heart that must be free to fly That burns with a need
to know the reason why
Why must we all conceal what we think and how we feel?
Must there be a secret me I'm forced to hide?
I won't pretend that I'm someone else for all time
When will my reflection show Who I am inside?*

Mulan struggled with being herself and having to please others. Have you ever felt like Mulan? I surely did. I struggled with indecision in my life because of fear of what others would think.

We all wear a mask sometimes. Sometimes we wear a mask for so long that we don't even recognize who we are. That is why self-awareness is so critical. Seeing yourself as you indeed are, is crucial to personal growth and development. Once you can see the truth, you can develop your natural talents and use your natural passions to find greater success and fulfillment.

> *"Knowing others is wisdom; knowing yourself is Enlightenment."*
> **~ Lao Tzu**

When you look at your reflection, what are you reflecting on? So often, we reflect on the wrong things. Sometimes we look at ourselves, and we get caught up measuring ourselves with someone else's ruler.

We get stuck on what we have or don't have and what we have done. As we reflect, we need to think of it like driving. If we keep our focus on what's in the rear-view mirror, we are sure to crash into something in front of us. When we reflect, it is good to take a quick glimpse at where we are; however, we need to focus on what is before us. The goal is to be the best version of yourself. Don't get stuck where you are. Keep it moving.

The dictionary defines self-awareness as "conscious knowledge of one's character, feelings, motives, and desires." It's the ability to see ourselves clearly, understand who we are, how others see us, and how we fit into the world. Self-awareness gives us power. Power to embrace and power to change. There's comfort in knowing ourselves.

One benefit of self-awareness is that it can influence your relationships, career, and happiness for the better. As you become more self-aware, you take control of your life. Self-awareness is the primary way of understanding and navigating your thoughts, beliefs, emotions, and reactions. As you become more self-aware, you will be able to highlight faulty, limiting beliefs and emotional responses that stand in your way. Becoming more aware of these reactions will give you the power to adjust. Self-awareness is the foundation for your personal progress.

HOW TO DEVELOP SELF-AWARENESS

You build your self-awareness one step at a time. Getting to know the real you will take time. There are all kinds of reports and documentaries out there on self-awareness. You can start to develop your self-awareness by asking yourself some simple questions. What are your goals? What are some of your dreams and desires? Writing down what is important to you is a significant first step for understanding yourself and your beliefs. You can also ask yourself what others might say about you? This doesn't mean you allow yourself to be limited by what others might say. This is just to get an idea of how those around you describe you. This can help you to see if the characteristic you feel you represent is accurately being perceived.

There are many that practice meditation to develop self-awareness. When I first read about meditation, I thought it was something complicated. I now incorporate it into my daily routines. I started meditating to destress by taking a moment to just breathe in and breathe out. I learned that as you meditate, it allows you to develop a better awareness of the present. Meditation is an ideal activity for enhancing self-awareness. If you practice this regularly, you'll find it helps you to clear your mind. It also allows you to pay attention to yourself, others, and your surroundings.

Question yourself throughout the day. "What do I want to achieve?" "What emotions do I feel right now, and what can I do to change them if I need to?"

> *"Who are you really?*
>
> *you are not a name*
> *or a height, or a weight*
> *or a gender*
> *you are not an age*
> *and you are not where you are from*
>
> *you are your favorite books*
> *and the songs stuck in your head*
> *you are your thoughts*
> *and what you eat for breakfast*
> *on Saturday mornings*
>
> *you are a thousand things*
> *but everyone chooses*
> *to see a million things*
> *you are not*
>
> *you are not*
> *where you are from*
> *you are where you are going*
> *and I'd like to go there too."*
> *— M.K.*

SO, WHO ARE YOU REALLY?

Queen, your identity is a powerful force in your life and speaks volumes to others who meet you. Your personal identity is made up of more than just your thoughts and feelings. There are plenty of psychological theories about what makes up our identity.

Many believe your personal family history is one of the biggest elements contributing to who you become. Things like who you grew up with, how you were raised, and the experiences you had from an infant's time all the way through your early adult years are powerful factors affecting the development of your personal identity. In essence, where you've come from plays a significant role in who you are; however, this doesn't define who you are. Your present identity isn't limited to your history. You can always take steps to be the person you want to be at any time.

> *"My past has not defined me, destroyed me, deterred me, or defeated me; it has only strengthened me."*
> *– Steve Maraboli*

Just as the people in your pasts contribute to who you are, the people you most closely affiliate with also contribute to who you are today. Have you ever heard the saying, "you are a sum total of the five closest people to you"? Usually, your friends share interests in the same kinds of things you find fascinating. Most people find themselves doing the same things their closest buddies do. If you are into fitness, most of your buddies are probably into fitness too. We generally gravitate towards people who share our similarities. Just like your family history, you are not restricted to your past circles. You can always be more selective about the people you hang out with. For example, if you want to be studious, you can hang out with people who spend time in libraries or like to study.

Your personal style and appearance can also provide a picture of who you are. Your clothes, hairstyle, and how you conduct yourself combine to make up an essential aspect of your identity. Your feelings, thoughts, and beliefs about you are the most important thing that makes you, YOU. How you feel about yourself as an individual makes up your self-image. What you believe about yourself is the greatest influence in determining your personal identity.

This brings to mind a story I heard about the lion and the sheep. I have seen this story start in various ways; however, they all teach the same thing. As the story goes, "There was once a baby lion left by its dying mother among some sheep. The sheep fed it and gave it shelter. The other sheep teased him as the lion grew because he didn't look the same or sound like the others. His "Ba-a-a" sounded a little different. One day another lion came by. All the sheep ran, including the sheep-lion.

The lion chased after the young cub. When he caught him, he asked, "What are you doing here?" said the older lion in astonishment: for he heard the sheep-lion trying to sound like the rest of the sheep. The young lion explained how he was frightened. "Nonsense!" roared the older iiilion, "come with me; I will show you." And he took him to the side of a smooth stream and showed him that which was reflected therein. "You are a lion; look at me, look at the sheep, look at yourself." And the sheep-lion looked, and then he said, "Ba-a-a, I do not look like the sheep — it is true, I am a lion!" and with that, he roared a roar that shook the hills to their depths.

For the first time, he became aware of who he was. He Crowned himself with self-awareness. He was a King. Likewise, realize who you are. You are a Queen.

"Believe in your infinite potential. Your only limitations are those you set upon yourself."
*— **Roy T. Bennett***

Queen, ponder who you are as an individual ruling your Queendom. Recognize that your identity is a complex mix of your history, affiliations, and thoughts and beliefs about you.

Don't let the expectations and opinions of other people affect your decisions. It's your life, not theirs. Do what matters most to you; do what makes you feel alive and happy. Don't let the expectations and ideas of others limit who you are. If you let others tell you who you are, you are living their reality — not yours. There is more to life than pleasing people. There is much more to life than following others' prescribed paths. There is so much more to life than what you experience right now. You need to decide who you are for yourself. Become a whole being. Adventure."
*— **Roy T. Bennett***

DISCOVERING YOUR PERSONAL SET OF VALUES

It is crucial to get in touch with your own values on your journey to honestly know yourself. It's easy to get distracted by other people's ideas. Sometimes you may even think that the ideas are your own until you get a clear understanding of your own set of principles and morals so you can stand firm in your beliefs.

Your values are simply the things at your core that are most important to you. They are the unwavering belief in what you stand for. When you know your values, you can live an authentic life doing what you truly desire. Take time to reflect on different areas of your life and ask yourself a few questions. For example, what are some of the things that are most important to you? Where do you see yourself living or working as you get older? Do you even see yourself working? Maybe you see yourself owning a business or doing volunteer or ministry work. Questions like these will help you discover your values.

Core values like spirituality, family, women's empowerment, and multicultural diversity are my top priorities. You may value many things in your life, as well. However, it is important to identify your highest priorities. Maybe relationships are amongst your top core values. This includes finding all relationships important, not just romantic ones. Often this means that you hold your interactions with your loved ones to be one of the most essential things in life. You may have a core value that highlights your commitment to religion or spiritual practice. Or perhaps one of the values you may enjoy is being creative and discovering new things. Maybe one of your core values includes finding a way to make your mark on the world.

Many times, finding out what genuinely makes you happy will help you identify your core values. So ask yourself, what are some of the things that bring you the most joy? The answers will lead you to your core values. If ever you feel like your life has taken a wrong turn, examine your core values to get you back on a path in the direction you'd like to go. That path will likely lead you to happiness!

CROWN YOURSELF AND DISCOVER YOUR TRUE PASSIONS

One of the most exciting parts of living authentically is getting to design your life around the things you love most! We just talked about your values. Now we'll add your passions to your quest for self-discovery. If you're lucky, you've already discovered your passions in life and have devoted much of your life to fulfilling dreams and goals related to things that bring you excitement and joy. However, sometimes, It takes time, soul-searching, and some life experience to identify your true passions. So, to get your thoughts, ideas, and desires flowing, explore the following questions.

What's the one thing you have always wanted to do since you were a child? I stated earlier that I wanted to do three things from the time I was 6 years old. I wanted to be a minister, get married, and be a millionaire. Those desires have contributed to my decisions throughout my life. It took me a while to understand my true core value and passion for these items. For example, my desire for marriage is related to my core value of quality relationships and my passion for my family. They are my "Why, my everything. Similarly, my entrepreneurial pursuits are driven by my desire to be a millionaire to provide for ministry and my family. What about you, is there something that has driven you from a young age?

What would you do if you could do whatever you wanted? Let your mind go. I have been told that when you do something you love and are passionate about, work doesn't feel like work.

Where do you really want to live? I have a friend that desires to be in a more secluded place. She always talks about being in a place to simply enjoy nature and avoid all the hustle and bustle of city life.

Can you imagine being in a place where you wake up to less stress every day just because of the place you live?

What is something you would like to explore that no one knows about? Perhaps you're harboring a secret yearning to write your own book. Maybe you have stories in you that can empower others. I have a mentor that says the best way to empower a woman is to give her a microphone. She masters in helping women to use their voices to change their situations and create wealth. You can make that happen too.

What do you talk about often? My husband had two lanes of conversations; one was ministry, and the other was sports. Anytime you heard him speak, his conversation would drift to either of those subjects. Football and ministry were in his blood. So much so that he had a next-level ministry series that helped high school students pursue their athletic and college careers. What about you? Is there something you find yourself talking about more than others?

Who supports you the most? Who are the people that will stand behind you and help you pursue your passions, no matter what? Similarly, who seems to block you from achieving your goals? It is important to differentiate between those who will encourage you and those who will discourage you. You might be required to leave some people behind or cut some loose to find your true passions.

What one thing could you change in your life right now that would make your life better? What's missing from your life? Answering these questions requires considerable soul-searching.

Your true passions are just waiting to be discovered! Finding your passions is one of the most enjoyable tasks in learning to live authentically. Knowing your passions helps clarify your self-concept.

> *"I want to encourage women to embrace their own uniqueness. Because just like a rose is beautiful, so is a sunflower, so is a peony. I mean, all flowers are beautiful in their own way, and that's like women too."*
> ~ ***Miranda Kerr***

CROWN YOURSELF BY USING AFFIRMATIONS

As you read through this book, some sections will be followed by a series of Affirmations. Affirmations are short, positive statements that can be read, repeated to yourself, or listened to from a recording. These statements can be used to improve your self-esteem, help you reach a goal, break a bad habit, or even discover more about yourself.

Many people believe that using affirmations can help you change how you view yourself and help you to reprogram your mind to think more positively about yourself. It may seem difficult at first if you're new to affirmations; however, there are just a few things to remember about using affirmations.

- Write affirmations in the present tense
- You can speak to yourself in the first person ('I") when you write or read your affirmations. (If you are looking at yourself in a mirror, you can use "you")
- Be short and concise to keep things simple.
- Read and write your affirmations when you're calm and away from distractions.
- Remember to stay positive and be sincerer.

Crown Yourself with Self-Awareness Affirmations

I discover more about myself each day

I identify my strengths and weaknesses

I strive to know and understand myself

I increase my awareness

I am committed to learning more about who I am

I am encouraged to continue growing and evolving

I find myself interesting. I want to know more

Reflections

PILLAR 3 – SELF ACCEPTANCE

CROWN YOURSELF WITH SELF-ACCEPTANCE

Queen, to live authentically, it's important that you not only know yourself but accept yourself as well. That means accepting your strengths, weaknesses, and all your flaws. As a mentor and life coach, I have talked with many women and teenagers that are often absorbed in comparing themselves to others. They sometimes have difficulty recognizing the treasures in their own life because they desire the glory they see in others. I often share with them an allegory I once heard. The story goes, "One day a King came to his garden and saw withering and dying trees, bushes and flowers. There was an Oak tree. He asked why it is dying? The oak said it dies because it can't be as high as a pine. The pine tree was also dying. It said it was falling down because it could not give grapes like a grapevine. The grapevine was determined to die because it could never stand tall and bear large fruit like the peach tree. The geranium was depressed because its flowers were not as tall and fragrant as the lilac.

The king continued walking through his garden, dismayed by its desolate state, when he came across a small violet. Its tiny frame was beautifully bright and full of life. The king told the small flower: "You look radiant! You don't seem to be the least disheartened about the misery and discouragement around you." The violet replied: "No, I am not. I know I'm small, but I imagine you would have planted it here instead of me if you wanted an oak tree or a pine tree where I am.

Since I know you wanted a violet, and I cannot be anything other than what I am, I try to develop my best qualities and be the best I can be. iv

The moral of the story is, look at yourself. You can only be you. You can't become someone else. You can enjoy life and blossom, or you can wither and die if you do not accept yourself. One of my favorite scriptures says, "You are fearfully and wonderfully made." It reminds me that I was made this way. It is my job to be the best me I can be.

Ask yourself a few questions: Do you say or do things to impress others? Do you say or do things to avoid being ridiculed by others? Do you work at a job that you don't like, so you can make more money to buy things you want or to impress others? The list of questions can go on forever. Often, we seek validation or the approval of others. However, the real secret to contentment is self-acceptance.

> *"The truth is: Belonging starts with self-acceptance. Your level of belonging, in fact, can never be greater than your level of self-acceptance because believing that you're enough is what gives you the courage to be authentic, vulnerable, and imperfect."*
> **– Brene Brown**

The first step to building self-esteem is accepting yourself. Self-acceptance is the level of happiness and satisfaction you have with yourself. You can't accept yourself if you don't feel positive about yourself.

It would be a mistake to think of self-acceptance as a blanket acceptance of your weaknesses, bad habits, and negative tendencies in the absence of any responsibility to continue to improve. Self-acceptance isn't an excuse for laziness and complacency. You can be content and still advocate self-improvement. It also doesn't mean that you accept your fate and determine that nothing can or should be done to change your life.

Queen, you must accept yourself for who you are and not who others want you to be. Self-acceptance is something we all wrestle with from time to time. It's an acknowledgment of our shortcomings, character, strengths, habits, and tendencies. It's about facing the truth about who we are and accepting that reality. It is just like using a navigation system to get directions. You must first accept where you are before you can map out where you are going.

You may go through times when you're unhappy with who you are as you learn to accept yourself. You may feel like you've underachieved with what you've attained in life. Or you may feel confused about which path you're taking. There may even be days when your best doesn't seem good enough to you, but don't get down on yourself. Come to terms with your true self and acknowledge the awesome person you are. Your various characteristics combine to make something totally unique and special. No one else has your individual talents. No one else could ever take your unique place in this world. You have greatness in you.

> *"There is nothing more rare, nor more beautiful, than a woman being unapologetically herself, comfortable in her perfect imperfection. To me, that is the true essence of beauty."*
> ~ ***Steve Maraboli***

CELEBRATING AND FORGIVING YOURSELF

To start accepting your true self and come to terms with who you are, know that you are special. You are a beautiful creation. You weren't made this way by mistake. Look at your beliefs, likes, and dislikes are all part of a magnificent design. I'll say it again, you were fearfully and wonderfully made.

Throughout your life, I'm sure you've achieved some things, both personally and professionally. You've had some victories, no matter how big or small. The fact that you are here and reading this book is an accomplishment in itself. You can celebrate that.

You're a winner by merit of what you've accomplished, and no one can take those victories away from you.

"I celebrate who I am, what I love, and all of my blessings that lead to joy."
— Amy Leigh Mercree

Learning to accept and celebrate yourself can be difficult during tough times. However, even when you have bad days, always try to look at the bright side. Try to find the good in every situation. I know some situations can feel absolutely devastating. Learning to have compassion for yourself and to accept the situation may take time. So often, the most difficult person for us to forgive is ourselves. We allow regret, shame, and guilt to prevent us from letting go of our past mistakes. It is important not to dwell on unfortunate times. Instead, we should reflect on our experience and learn from it to move forward. If we refuse to forgive ourselves of our regrets, we remain trapped in the past.

"Bring it up, make amends, forgive yourself. It sounds simple, but don't think for a second that it is easy. Getting free from the tyranny of past mistakes can be hard work but definitely worth the effort. And the payoff is health, wholeness, and inner peace. In other words, you get your life back."
*– **Steve Goodier***

YOU CAN LET GO OF PAST MISTAKES AND MOVE FORWARD

It is tough to overcome something if you aren't willing to learn from it and hold yourself accountable. You have to be willing to take 100% responsibility for what is happening in your life. Identify what you did or didn't do and own up to it instead of justifying your actions. Being honest with yourself by stating where you went wrong will release the pain, guilt, and shame you feel. Examine the events and circumstances and be honest about how you felt then and are feeling now. If others were affected, you can try to remedy the situation and make amends, offer an apology, and ask for forgiveness. This action alone can be very healing for both you and the person that suffered harm because of your mistake.

One of the best things to do is share your story with others so that they might be able to avoid making the same mistake. Realize that you've grown, and you're no longer the same person that made the original mistake. You can use your story to help others to avoid similar situations in the future. We all make mistakes. Sometimes they come with unavoidable consequences.

Regardless, we all deserve forgiveness, no matter how serious our errors might have been. Sometimes even though you let go of your mistakes, the guilt remains. Feelings of guilt can be distressing and draining. It is important to get over the guilt and move forward.

Learn from the mistake and the guilt you feel. After you know why you feel guilty, you can now benefit and learn from it. You can visualize yourself behaving in a new and improved manner. Realize the guilt is unproductive and acknowledge your feelings and the pain that goes with them. Accept that you made a mistake and realize that it will pass. As you Forgive yourself, make sure to let it go. However, learn from your mistakes and go forward with a new perspective and strategy. Apologize and forgive yourself.

> *"Stop focusing on your past mistakes. Don't be ashamed of the things that you've done. We ALL have made mistakes. Don't you see? All of those things helped shape you into the beautiful person that you are today! Hold your head up high because you didn't allow your past mistakes to consume you. You learned! You conquered! You became a better YOU. Be proud of who you are TODAY!"*
> *— Stephanie Lahart*

Challenging yourself to do better is the crucial final step to self-forgiveness. After you accept your imperfections, take time to work at fixing the things you can. It might not happen overnight; however, you can work at making things right over time. What is most important is that you commit to turning things around and forgive yourself. You're full of so much potential. That potential sits unused while you consume yourself with negative energy. Lift yourself up! Come to terms with the fact that you have so much more to give to the world. Chip away at the negativity until all that's left is your renewed spirit.

TURN YOUR INNER CRITIC INTO YOUR PERSONAL CHEERLEADER

It can be easy to beat yourself up over your shortcomings and failures. Your inner critic attempts to protect you, but it's causing more harm than good, like an overprotective parent. Criticizing yourself only makes life more challenging for you. It puts limits on your life and robs you of options. You don't have to listen to the information your inner critic provides. Sometimes your inner critic can be relentless. It is active from when you wake up until you go to sleep; even in your dreams, that inner critic is active! I know for me that inner critic has been one of the hardest things to contain. Give yourself some grace to recover from your mistakes. Stop the negative conversations we have with ourselves! You can't continue to live in the past, rehashing what you did or didn't do. Start living in the present.

CHANGE YOUR SELF TALK AND REACH YOUR FULL POTENTIAL

When you hear that negative talk cancel it and replace it with positive talk IMMEDIATELY. Replace the negative talk in your mind with positive talk and imagery. Don't give your inner critic any chance to create roadblocks for you. Jack Canfield teaches to say "Cancel-Cancel" to get rid of it in your conscious mind and get rid of it in your subconscious mind as well. As you practice keeping your self-talk positive, expect great things to happen. The truth of the matter is your inner critic is a manifestation of your fear. Its purpose is to stop you from harming yourself. However, it's like a scared child. Fear is False Evidence Appearing Real.

"There is no illusion greater than fear."
~ Lao Tzu

It is said, "Feel the fear and do it anyway." If there is something you need to get done, just get started and do it. The thoughts that try to stop you from getting things done will clear up as you get busy. You keep your critic at bay as you get into action. It is the best way to calm the chatter in your mind. As you get going, you'll find it wasn't as bad as you thought after all.

If you need some extra encouragement, think about what a GOOD FRIEND would tell you. Would they judge you as harshly as you judge yourself? If the situation was reversed, what would you say? How would you encourage them? Be your own best friend. Treat yourself just as kindly as you would your best friend. You can say something encouraging to yourself every 10 minutes if you have to. You can use a timer to get into the habit of encouraging yourself regularly. Just think, after 18 hours, you would have said over 100 positive things to yourself. Now that's encouragement. We'll talk about forming habits later, but you'll have created this positive habit in no time at this rate. Criticizing yourself is a habit. Encouraging yourself is also a habit. You just need to determine which one you will do.

Get in the habit of encouraging yourself and celebrating your successes. It can be easy fixating on a few bad choices instead of celebrating your triumphs. Make a choice to focus on your greatest achievements and review them regularly. Watch how your mood is enhanced and how you turn that critic into a cheerleader.

As you continue your self-acceptance journey, it's important to learn how to get past your doubts. These doubts can destroy your confidence and make you feel like you're less than you really are, just like your inner critic limits your life and your opportunities.

Having poor self-esteem or a lack of self-confidence can be extremely damaging to your life. Your perception of yourself is your self-image. Whether you think of yourself as intelligent or lazy, your beliefs about yourself can be liberating or constricting. Your decisions and your ability to succeed can be limited or influenced by your self-image. A negative self-image can have you doubting yourself and your gifts and talents. If you believe that you have what you need inside you, you'll enjoy more of what you desire in life.

REMEMBER YOU ARE ENOUGH!
You have what it takes. You are strong enough. You are brave enough. You are capable enough. You are worthy enough. Is time to stop thinking otherwise and start believing in yourself because no one else has the dreams you have. No one else sees the world exactly like you do, and no one else holds the same magic inside. It's time to start believing in the power of your dreams, my beautiful friend. Not next year, not next month, not tomorrow, but now you are ready. You are enough.

*- **Nikki Banas***

OVERCOMING THE WIZARD OF OZ SYNDROME

Have you ever allowed self-doubt to keep you from achieving something you wanted? I did. One of my mentors once told me I suffered from the Wizard of Oz Syndrome. I was baffled at what he said. He explained that Dorothy wanted to go home in The Wizard of Oz, the Scarecrow wanted a brain, the Tin Man wanted a heart, and the Lion wanted courage. They all believed that the great and powerful Oz could give them what they wanted. My mentor told me that I already had everything I needed, just like Dorothy, the Scarecrow, the Tin Man, and the Lion. They possessed what they each were in search of, and so did I. Like in the Wizard of Oz, we often look for someone else to give us what we already have or do for us that we can do ourselves. Sometimes we don't recognize the power we possess. We each are unique and possess a great and powerful gift.

You already have what you need to be your best self. The first thing you need to do is, see it. As we have been discussing the importance of self-awareness and acceptance. Recognize and acknowledge the full reality of your situation, and don't run from it. Deal with it. This will take courage, and just like the Cowardly Lion, you have it in you. It takes courage to step into your Queendom and rule your life.

Many of us have stories to tell, hurts and pains, and excuses that hold us captive as victims of our situations. Instead, like the Tinman, we need to examine our hearts and take ownership of our problems to help others. Realize you are the healing that someone else needs. Remember that your mess can become a message and be the word someone else needs to be free.

We have within us the power to change our reality by acknowledging and accepting our shortcomings and beginning to move in the direction of the life we desire. Just like the Scarecrow seeking a brain, this step requires you to think about the desire you would like to see and creatively plan the route to reach your destination. The solution was there all along, for Dorothy, the scarecrow, the tinman, and the lion.

Realize you are enough; you have everything you need inside of you. My pastor, Bishop Russell Smyre, used the definition of a few Latin words to break down the word Education in one of his messages. He explained, "The word 'education' has been derived from Latin words-'Educar,' 'Educare' and 'Educatum.' **'Educar'**- The term 'educar' means to bring up, rise, and nourish, train or mold. **'Educare'**- 'educare' means 'to lead out,' 'to draw out,' and 'bring forth.' **'Educatum'** is composed of two terms, "E" and "Duco." "E" implies a movement from inward to outward, and "Duco" means developing and progressing. Education is therefore bringing forth what is already in you and being made manifest outside of you. Cultivate and nourish the things you have inside." As we grow in knowledge and education, we bring forth what's inside. You already have what you need.

"Always keep your mind strong with thoughts of positivity; your head up with full confidence and a big smile on your face because you truly have greatness in you."
*~ **Edmond Mbiaka***

Crown Yourself with Self-Acceptance Affirmations

I am enough.

I am proud of the person I am now and the one I am growing into

My beauty shines from the inside out and creates a glow.

I accept myself – wholly and completely

My commitment is to become the best possible version of myself

I am my biggest advocate

I look in the mirror and see a divine creation

Reflections

PILLAR 4 – RIGHT MINDSET

CROWN YOURSELF WITH THE RIGHT MINDSET

As we have discussed, the first step to living a better life starts with self-awareness and self-acceptance. Believing you have everything you need and that you are enough. Your mindset is the foundation from which everything else evolves. Without the proper mindset, your efforts will be negatively affected.

How many of you have ever had that conversation in your mind that really criticize you for making mistakes or making bad choices from time to time? You know that conversation that goes a little like, "YOU KNOW YOU SHOULDN'T HAVE EATEN THAT; YOU KEEP SAYING YOU'RE GOING TO CHANGE YOUR EATING HABITS, YOU ALWAYS DO THIS, YOU LACK DISCIPLINE, YOU NEED TO BE STRICTER ON YOURSELF." Or "YOU SAID YOU WERE GONNA GET THOSE EMAILS OUT, YOU SAID YOU WERE GONNA MAKE 10 CALLS, YOU..." You make a simple mistake, and you tend to beat yourself up for it…and your mind goes all-in on why and how you blew it!v

Your thoughts, attitudes, and self-talk are all important components of your mindset. Just as important is your comfort level with living your best life. Not everyone is comfortable with the idea of great success. Eliminate your fears of failure and raise your success ceiling. You can accomplish more when you aren't afraid of failing. A positive attitude can make all the difference and affects your efforts in multiple ways. With a success-oriented mindset, any goal is possible.

HOW LIMITING BELIEFS AFFECT YOUR LIFE

"Since a leader cannot rise above his thinking, he must assault his limiting beliefs daily thru reading, listening & associating."
*– **Orrin Woodward***

Some have used excuses as justifications for remaining stuck in their current circumstances. The excuse used is a form of limiting belief. Your various limiting beliefs impact your attitude, actions, and results. Limiting beliefs are thoughts and opinions that stop us from being our best selves. These beliefs cause you to feel inadequate. They hold you back from attaining your desirable options or your happiness. Your limiting beliefs can have more of a negative impact on your life than any other factor. These beliefs short-circuit your success. It will be tough to complete your goals with limiting beliefs. Most people won't take any action they think is doomed to fail. You're likely to quit trying as soon as you believe it won't work.

If you think you are beaten, you are,
If you think you dare not, you don't.
If you like to win, but you think you can't,
It is almost certain you won't.

If you think you'll lose, you're lost
for out of the world we find,
Success begins with your will—
It's all in the state of mind.

If you think you are outclassed, you are,
You've got to think high to rise.
You've got to be sure of yourself before
You can ever win the prize.

Life's battles don't always go
To the stronger or faster person,
But sooner or later, the one who wins
is the one who THINKS HE CAN!
*~**Napoleon Hill**vi*

Limiting beliefs not only prevent your success but also negatively affect your life in other ways. It taints your experience of living, and you affect others around you with your limiting beliefs. There is a story that my husband used to illustrate how your beliefs can hold you back.

The story begins with a man who was walking through the grounds of a circus. He noticed something interesting in one area. All the elephants were secured only with a small rope that was tied around one of their ankles. They didn't have chains, nor fences, nor any other deterrent—just this small rope. The man thought it was strange because elephants can weigh anywhere from 5000 to 14,000 pounds. He realized the elephants could easily break these ropes and go stampeding through the circus crowd.

The man asked the trainer why the elephants didn't try to break free and escape. The trainer explained that when the elephants are young and smaller, they use these same ropes to tie them up. At that age, the rope is strong enough to hold them. At first, the elephants will try to break free, but they quickly learn they're powerless, and eventually, they're conditioned to believe that it's impossible to break free from the rope. viiAs adults, they think the rope can still hold them, so they don't even try.

These elephants can pull up whole trees with their trunks, yet they will remain in captivity held by only a light rope, despite their ability to easily break away. They don't even try. Why?

Because after trying and trying as a young elephant to break free, suddenly something attaches itself to them stronger than any rope or chain or fence. It's the belief that they can't. That belief holds them back despite their ability.

Have you ever had a belief like this that held you back as these ropes? I had one of those beliefs that prevented me from leaving an abusive marriage. These beliefs held me back and led me to feel unfulfilled, and I struggled in my relationship. I found myself living a life that was far from the one I wanted to have. It wasn't until I became aware of the ropes holding me and actively pulled against them that I found myself able to break free.

"Beliefs have the power to create and the power to destroy. Human beings have the awesome ability to take any experience of their lives and create a meaning that disempowers them or one that can literally save their lives."-
Tony Robbins

By now, you probably can start to name a few ropes that hold you back. The limiting beliefs we carry around come from various sources in our lives. Fortunately, you can replace limiting beliefs with beliefs to empower you. Understanding where these limiting beliefs come from will be important as you deal with the roadblocks in your life. It is important to recognize these sources. Some of these sources might surprise you. Many of these sources were trying to help you, so don't blame them. They simply believed the wrong things, too.

SOURCES OF LIMITING BELIEFS

Many of our limiting beliefs come from family, although they may mean well. Think about the things your mom or dad told you couldn't be done. I'm sure they meant well. Unfortunately, many times our family taught us out of their own limited experiences. There may have been statements like; there is never enough, or money doesn't grow on trees. These beliefs may hinder your ability to achieve wealth. Maybe you grew up in an economically challenged lifestyle, so you believed that being wealthy was impossible for you. Much like our families, friends can do and say things that lead us to believe we're less capable than we are as well. Teachers also have a lot of influence over us. I remember a teacher that literally kicked a chair across the room as he told me that "I would never be an engineer" because I was swimming with two bowling balls. One being a minority and the other being a woman. I could have let that stop me; however, instead, it became my driving force. I wanted to prove him wrong.

A similar story of a young girl who almost gave up on her dreams because of a teacher. The young girl was 17. She loved writing and telling stories. From the time she was about 4 years old, she wanted to be a storyteller. All through her schooling, her teachers encouraged her. She entered the school of journalism in college. It was recommended that she complete the honors course.

She wrote her first short story then, and before it was to be presented to the class, the professor called her into his office to discuss her story. He took her manuscript and threw it across his desk. He told her that her writing stinks. She was devastated. She had banked her whole life on being a storyteller. He told her she had no plot structure or characterization concept and that there was no way she'd ever make it as a writer. He made a bargain with her that he wouldn't fail her but rather would give her a "B" if she'd promise never to write again. She realized that she was giving up on her dreams.

For 14 years, this young girl didn't write anything and took on the limiting belief that she was a poor storyteller. One year while her family was on vacation, there were producers, journalists, directors, and a group of writers sitting around one of the tables at the pool. She told them her secret dream was to be a writer. One of the older guys told her that, "If you wanted to be a writer, you would be a writer." She told them about the professor and that he said she had no talent. He gave her his card and told her to call him if she did some writing. She went home and wrote a book.

The authors' name is Catherine Lanigan, and the book she wrote was "Romancing the Stone." Since then, she has written over 21 books.

This story is important because it illustrates that you have the greatest influence on your limiting beliefs. People will tell you what you can't do. It is up to you if you choose to believe them. viii

I saw a video where Jack Canfield told a woman her hair was green. He explained to the audience that she didn't get upset about what he said because she knew her hair wasn't green. He then said she was one of the most selfish people he'd ever met in his life. He explained that if she was to get upset, it wouldn't be because of what he said, but instead her belief about herself before saying anything. It only triggers the emotion if you're already worried about it; otherwise, you'd just dismiss it as false. Likewise, your interpretation of what your parents, friends, or teachers say to you creates your limiting beliefs. For example, if your parent told you, *"You could never get into college."* You could choose to believe that, or you could believe, "I can do it if I want to do it." It's all up to you. Consider all the sources of information and opinions in your life. They all could steer you in the wrong direction. Have you ever been told that you can't accomplish something because of skin color, gender, or another differentiating factor? Sometimes these statements can put us in a box that is difficult to break out of; nevertheless, you can break free of other people's limiting beliefs.

> *"It's so important to identify beliefs. Because once you identify [a negative belief], once you bring it into the light, you will see it doesn't belong to you: - That it came from your parents; - It came from your family; - It came from your society; - It came from your friends. And you bought into it. But it isn't yours.*
> *Holding on to something that isn't yours is called theft.*
> *Don't be a belief thief!*
> *Let go of what isn't yours."*
> ~ ***Bashar***

DISCOVERING YOUR LIMITING BELIEFS

Before you can change anything, you first must identify it. Examine the areas in your life that you are not satisfied with. Are you actively doing something to fix those areas? Your beliefs affect your behavior. You can't change your actions until you change your thinking. For Example, your finances. Do you feel financial pressure in your life? What about your relationships? Are your relationships satisfying? Are there any areas of your life you're experiencing dissatisfaction? List your beliefs, good or bad, for any area you are dissatisfied with.

_____

_____

_____

_____

_____

_____

_____

Which of these beliefs do you feel may create the most challenge in your life? Which of these beliefs may cause the greatest negative impact on your life? After you've identified your limiting beliefs, let's start to eliminate them.

ELIMINATE LIMITING BELIEFS

After you've identified your limiting belief, like negative self-talk, get rid of it IMMEDIATELY. Tell yourself, you choose not to believe that anymore. Stating your intention has a profound effect on your mindset. Jack Canfield, the author of Chicken Soup for the Soul, teaches you should say, "Cancel-Cancel," and then replace it with what you now believe. Like the example earlier, if you know your hair is brown, you won't believe someone who tries to convince you it is green.

Create a new belief that serves your desired outcome. Find examples to support this new belief. Beliefs are more stable when there is supporting information and evidence.

Check your progress and how you feel about your new belief. Your subconscious is a direct link to your gut. As your beliefs change, your behavior should change. Our feelings and lives are a manifestation of our beliefs. Your life will change if your beliefs have really changed. Keep working through your list of negative beliefs. New limiting beliefs will show up as you experience new things. New challenges will present themselves as you set new goals. The limiting beliefs you have will change as you learn and experience more. It's like pulling weeds. You have to continue to examine your life for limiting beliefs and eliminate them. Some weeds continue to pop up over time, no matter what you do. Once you recognize them, simply get rid of them. Get rid of the self-created obstacles and self-limiting thought patterns you face. Take control of your thoughts and create new, empowering patterns.

"If you develop the absolute sense of certainty that powerful beliefs provide, then you can get yourself to accomplish virtually anything, including those things that other people are certain are impossible."
- William Lyon Phelps

Crown Yourself with MINDSET AFFIRMATIONS

My beliefs drive my positive behavior.

I turn my errors into learning experiences.

I am free of self-limiting beliefs

I choose to believe in myself.

I eliminate the root of negative mindsets

I attract other positive thinkers to my life

I only entertain ideas that are in line with who I truly am

I ponder good things that will influence me.

Reflections

PILLAR 5 – GOOD HABITS

CROWN YOURSELF BY FORMING EMPOWERING HABITS

We have talked about being self-aware and accepting who we are and the mindset to design the life you desire. Next, you'll need to form empowering habits to continue on your journey to living a better life. As you form new habits, you encourage your intentions and behaviors, both consciously and subconsciously. The likelihood of getting something done goes up dramatically when you intend to get it done. Your life becomes what you consistently do.

> *"Habits to us is as recipes are to food. If you're not enjoying your life, find new recipes."*
> ~ ***Sotero M Lopez II***

WHAT IS SO IMPORTANT ABOUT FORMING HABITS?

When you think about it, your life is all about the habits you have; your habits=your life. What you do every single day repeatedly combines, over time, to become the very foundation of your life. Habits are automatic behaviors. I once heard a professor explain how 95% of our activities are controlled by our subconscious mind. Only 5% is controlled by our conscious mind. However, we can program our subconscious. When you develop a habit, it takes that action out of the realm of making a conscious choice every time you do it.

Once it's a habit, you don't have to think about it or make yourself do something. It becomes automatic. There are both empowering and inhibiting habits. You are more likely to enjoy the life you want if you form positive habits.

The most basic elements of your life are your habits. Whether you look at your day-to-day routines or your overall life, it's made up of all the behaviors you do. Those actions practiced consistently are your habits.

"I never could have done what I have done without the habits of punctuality, order, and diligence, without the determination to concentrate on one subject at a time."
~Charles Dickens

THE SCIENCE OF HABIT DEVELOPMENT

Over the years, I have read a lot about how long it takes to create new positive behaviors. You'll hear that it takes anywhere from 10 to 28 days to establish a habit. However, some new research by Phillippa Lally and others at University College London has found that a behavior must be repeated 66 times consecutively before forming a habit.

Lally and the other researchers showed you're more likely to form a habit when you keep doing a behavior in the same place or situation. They showed that forming a new habit can depend on one of 2 types of cues: situational and contextual. Situational cues originate from your environment or location, and contextual cues are other behaviors that trigger the new behavior you wish to perform. An example of a situational cue is what you see in the morning when you first enter your kitchen: you see your coffeemaker and decide to make some coffee. Therefore, your coffee maker is something that triggers you to make and drink your morning coffee, which you do every morning. An example of a contextual cue would be that you head to the kitchen to prepare your morning coffee as soon as you shut off the alarm and put on your robe. Getting up and getting on your robe triggers you to go get coffee.

The research emphasizes the importance of consistency in behavior when trying to form a habit. After consistently doing the new behavior 66 times, you'll likely discover you're automatically performing the behaviors. You will have formed a habit. The research revealed that it helped to pair the new behavior with the one you already do regularly. For example, lay the package of floss right by your toothpaste tube or even on top of it to be reminded to do it just after you brush your teeth for the night if you want to create a habit of flossing your teeth. I actually tried this with the habit of drinking water.
I wanted to increase my water intake, and it was suggested to have a glass of water before you go to bed and once you wake up. I sat two bottles of water on my nightstand next to my alarm clock. This way, I would drink one bottle when I plugged my phone up at night before I went to bed and the other when my alarm clock went off as soon as I woke up.

"Good habits are the key to all success. Bad habits are the unlocked door to failure."
— Og Mandino

ELIMINATE HABITS THAT SMOTHER YOUR DREAMS

Habits can make your goals happen quickly, or they can slow you down. Your goals might never come true with poor habits. That's why it's so important to manage your habits. Many bad habits are procrastination techniques. We all seem to have a bad habit or two that we struggle with. Whether to eliminate our debt, get healthier, or stop drinking or smoking, there's always that one challenge we can't seem to beat. Even in the Bible, Paul talked about a thorn in his flesh that he continually had to deal with.

I was in a seminar that taught that bad habits result from us not handling our stress and boredom effectively and healthily. Many of our bad habits are simply ways that we've learned to deal with being stressed or bored. Do you recognize any of your bad habits? Can you see how that habit doesn't really accomplish anything other than making you feel better temporarily? Dealing with your stress or boredom may actually be caused by deeper issues. These issues can be tough to deal with; however, you must be honest if you're serious about making changes. Being more self-aware and accepting are critical to eliminating bad habits. Ask yourself if certain beliefs or reasons are behind the bad habits. Is there something deeper, a fear, an event, or a limiting belief causing you to hold on to something bad for you? It is crucial to recognize the causes of your bad habits to overcome them.

The solution for bad habits is simply to replace them with something healthier and more productive. You can choose to go for a run every time you get bored instead of eating junk food. You could find something other than shopping to help you feel better when you're feeling down. You can choose to get started on a project instead of procrastinating. Once you understand that bad habits address certain needs in your life, it will be easier to replace your bad habits with healthier behavior.

When you are faced with the stress or boredom that prompts your bad habit, you will need to plan how you will respond. Have you noticed what precedes your bad habit? You can use that trigger to start making your new habit. Notice what happens immediately before you have the urge to engage in that bad habit. Become an expert on your patterns. You greatly increase your likelihood of success by tackling one bad habit at a time.

Find something you enjoy doing, and you'll have a better chance of sticking to it. If you don't like going for a walk, it won't be effective to use it as a new habit. Learning to deal with stress and boredom effectively is key to becoming more successful and accomplishing your goals. Bad habits are not only a waste of time, but they also take us further from our desired destination.

Your life is headed in the wrong direction when you have poor habits to deal with stress, anxiety, and boredom. These habits can derail you. Find a more effective way to deal with your emotional discomfort, and the quality of your life will improve dramatically. Getting started is always the hardest part; however, just get started immediately and replace one bad habit with a better one.

HABITS THAT INCREASE THE LIKELIHOOD OF SUCCESS

Even if you only attack one habit a month, that's 12 habits in a year. That's enough to make a monumental difference in your life. Now we're going to put the focus on positive habits. Good habits create a positive mindset. When you focus on behaviors that you can control, you can develop plans and take action. Developing and keeping good habits is about the process over the result. Success takes time, and habits repeat themselves over time. Your individual habits serve to either move you closer to success or make success more challenging.

"First we form habits, then they form us. Conquer your bad habits, or they'll eventually conquer you."
~ Rob Gilbert

Og Mandino said, "I will form good habits and become their slave. And how will I accomplish this difficult feat? Through these scrolls, it will be done, for each scroll contains a principle which will drive a bad habit from my life and replace it with one which will bring me closer to success." We each need to take on more positive, enriching habits. Here are a few suggested habits to add to your life and increase your success.

-

Make sure to prioritize sleep. Prioritizing sleep has been a great challenge for me. The stress of the day made it difficult for me to lay down and go to sleep. Have you ever laid down, and your mind was on overdrive? A lack of sleep can cause you to be too groggy the next day and negatively impact your health.

Not everybody is the same, so if you need a full eight hours, make sure to get in bed early enough to get those hours. Many claim to do fine on 4-6 hours of sleep, but recent studies have shown that no one is as effective with 6 hours of sleep as 7.

Review your schedule nightly. Start to prepare for your next day tonight. Preparing for your tomorrow gets your subconscious mind to work on ideas and solutions. Identify your top three priorities and the top three people you need to connect with for your next day. Identifying your top priorities can help you stay focused. Instead of trying to complete all ten items on your to-do list, focus on the top three. The 80/20 rule says that 80% of your results are from 20% of your activity. Focus on the 20%. Also, identify the top three people that you need to contact. These contacts may be personal, work, or business-related. For me, one of those people was my Grandmother. I purposed to call her at least once a day, even if it was only for 5 minutes. She once told me that those 5 minutes made her day and gave her strength. It might be someone you need to inspire or someone that inspires you.

Create a daily shut-down routine. Your daily shutdown process ensures that you can get your sanity back at the end of your day.

Your approach doesn't need to be more than 10-15 minutes, and it can help you move successfully from work mode into a personal mode. It can be challenging to move into a personal mode when we have so much stuff going on at work. Make sure that you're unplugging from work in a noticeable and precise way. Unplugging from work enables you to create better boundaries, readjust your energy, and focus on the things in your life that mean the most to you, like your family and your community.

Rate your day. Review your day and acknowledge your successes and failures. This is an effective way to avoid making the same errors over and over. Rate your day, was it "ok," "great," or do you want a "do-over." "How could you have improved your day?" Your night routine allows you to reprogram and prepare yourself to be ready for your day tomorrow.

Skip the Phone. Many of you may use your phone as an alarm clock; however, fight the urge to have it be the first thing you interact with when you wake. After turning off the alarm, it is easy to check Facebook, other social media accounts, texts, or emails. Checking these first thing in the morning can get you running in all different directions. As soon as you check your mail or social media, you are giving control of your day over to someone or something else. Remember, you already reprogrammed your night and planned for your day. Work on your plan.

Start Your Day with Something Positive. A survey showed that watching just three minutes of negative news in the morning made people 27% more likely to have a bad day. Stay away from negative news first thing in the morning. It's good to be aware and know the world's happenings, but don't allow that negativity to impact your attitude and negatively impact those around you. There is a computer equation that is GI=GO. In programming, the equation means Garbage In equals Garbage Out. Well, it also means Good In equals Good Out. What you put in will come out. Simply blocking the negative and putting something good can produce excellent results. Find something, a song, a motivational video, meditation, pray, or devotion that you can help you to start your day off right.

Make meditation or prayer a part of your day. It is important to get in touch with your spirituality. This will help your creativity and your overall balance in life. Just fifteen minutes daily can provide a nice break and the opportunity to regroup.

Practice mindfulness. Mindfulness is practicing being present. It is aware of your surroundings and thoughts. It is keeping your mind on the task at hand and not worrying about the future.

Exercise daily. Exercise not only strengthens your health but also improves your alertness and self-esteem. The vast majority of successful people report exercising each day, rain or shine. It doesn't matter when you exercise, but most high achievers make time in the morning.

List 3 things you are grateful for! Have an attitude of gratitude. I believe this is the real magic. Find three things you are thankful for today. We will cover this more in-depth in the next section.

Crown Yourself with
EMPOWERING HABITS AFFIRMATIONS

I create routines that make me happy and healthy

I create priorities and focus on making one change at a time

I set specific goals

I have the power to transform any aspect of my life with new habits

The quality of my life is determined by the quality of my habits

I release myself from my bad habits

I am developing new and positive habits

Reflections

PILLAR 6 –GRATITUDE

CROWN YOURSELF WITH GRATITUDE

So far, we have touched on being your true authentic self and how a positive mindset and habits will help you live a better life. Now we will discuss what I believe is one of the greatest catalysts for change in our lives, gratitude. When we show appreciation, it is one of the highest emotional states. Unfortunately, we are a culture conditioned to focus on what we don't have rather than appreciating what we've already received. So often, we find ourselves complaining and talking about what we lack. Many people find it difficult to have what is often referred to as an attitude of gratitude. We will examine why you must take the time to appreciate even the smallest blessings to activate your gratitude by acknowledging the gifts in your life. Being grateful may not change your situation; however, it does change you. I have heard it said, if you change yourself, you can change the world.

Gratefulness makes us happy. There are people we know who seem to have everything, yet they are still unhappy. Then some have suffered loss and misfortune, and they seem to be happy even still. It has been said that gratefulness makes the difference. So, it is not happiness that makes us grateful; instead, gratefulness makes us happy.

> *"The more you are grateful for what you have, the more you can live fully in the present. When you live in the present moment, the greater you can build stepping stones for a brighter future."*
> *— Dana Arcuri*

You'll experience more power in your life the more you cultivate gratitude. The power to change is in having an attitude of gratitude. It is the very way we experience life. You can transform your health, both mental and physical, with gratefulness. You can also transform your spirituality and work to attract good things in your life with gratefulness.

WHAT IS GRATEFULNESS?

•

"Gratitude makes sense of our past, brings peace for today, and creates a vision for tomorrow."
- Melody Beattie

It is important to understand what gratefulness is and how it works to grow in gratefulness. I heard a message that gratefulness is equated to how it feels to experience something valuable to us that is just given to us. It is at the point where these two factors come together. Something we value is given to you, and you realize it's a real gift. You haven't bought it, you haven't earned it, you haven't traded for it, and you haven't worked for it. It is something that is just given to you. Gratefulness results from two factors: recognizing that something of value is freely given to you and responding to it. Robert Emmons, a leading scientific expert on gratitude, puts it this way, "gratitude has two key components. First, he writes, "it's an affirmation of goodness. We affirm that there are good things in the world, gifts, and benefits we've received." In the second part of gratitude, he explains, "We recognize that the sources of this goodness are outside of us. Gratitude needs to become a part of the way we live. We need to live grateful lives.

"Gratitude is a powerful catalyst for happiness. It's the spark that lights a fire of joy in your soul."
*~ **Amy Collette***

GRATITUDE AND A SPECIAL KIND OF HAPPINESS

As I stated earlier, living with an attitude of gratitude moves us toward happiness. A happiness that comes from within instead of the kind that depends on external events. A happiness that we are truly fulfilled with. This happiness comes with the opportunity to grow and to learn. Your gratitude is a state in which you are open to receive good things. You are open, receptive, and willing to receive abundance. And when you receive those exceptionally good things, you consistently and instinctively give thanks. In other words, gratitude is not a one-time event where you simply say, "Thank you."

Gratitude is a habit. It's a perpetual way of life, almost like breathing. You take in something good and breathe out gratitude. Harvard Medical School defines gratitude as ixa thankful appreciation for what an individual receives, whether tangible or intangible. With gratitude, people acknowledge the goodness in their lives. Being grateful is like a magnifying glass that highlights the good in our lives and minimizes the things we're unhappy about. Gratefulness enables us to see just how many good things we have in our lives. On the flip side, when we're not regularly grateful, we become discontent and unhappy with the way things are going. Gratefulness and contentment go together, which is one of the reasons it's so powerful. It's important to activate your gratitude by acknowledging the gifts most people take for granted. When you're grateful, it is difficult to complain or be angry or frustrated. You only have room for gratefulness.

> *"Happiness cannot be traveled to, owned, earned, worn, or consumed. Happiness is the spiritual experience of living every minute with love, grace, and gratitude."*
> **– Denis Waitley**

The more grateful you are, the better person you become. Eileen Caddy said, Gratitude helps you grow and expand; gratitude brings joy and laughter into your life and the lives of all those around you. Do you want to grow and expand? Do you want to bring joy and laughter into the lives of those around you? Do you want to become the absolute best version of yourself that you can possibly be?

Let's be clear, being grateful doesn't mean that you don't work hard or seek to make money or to be more successful. It simply means that you're extremely thankful for what you have. And here's the paradox…The more grateful you are, the more likely you will work harder and produce more good things in your life.

THE POWER OF GRATITUDE

Gratitude changes our perspective, our outlook, and our feelings. It can even change how we express ourselves. As a result, gratitude changes our experiences. Research has even shown that gratitude has the power to heal, the power to energize, and the power to change lives. In fact, people have reported a healing power of gratefulness that can heal them of past hurts and give them hope and inspiration for the future. They reported it represents a change in mindset, to focus on what someone has instead of what they are lacking or deprived of.

"Gratitude is one of the most powerful human emotions. Once expressed, it changes attitude, brightens outlook, and broadens our perspective."
— ***Germany Kent***

THE SCIENCE OF GRATITUDE

We've talked about the feel-good side of gratitude. The scientific evidence has also shown that an attitude of gratitude can measurably improve your overall well-being. The Clinical Psychology Review-Journal, Gratitude and Well-Being: A Review and Theoretical integration said that practicing gratitude is good for you and your loved one. It noted that people who practice being grateful get sick less often. Studies showed that 10% fewer stress-related illnesses were in people that practice being grateful. They have healthier hearts. It also showed 10% to 16% of people had lower blood pressure and exercised 1.5 hours per week more. Also, studies show that those who practice gratitude slept 10% longer and 15% better. They were more optimistic and overcame adversity 23% more. Gratitude lowers levels of the stress hormone cortisol. They said that gratitude kickstarts the production of dopamine and serotonin in our brain.

It is almost like an anti-depressant, producing feel-good neurotransmitters creating feelings of happiness and contentment.

Just like you can strengthen your body's muscles, you can also build gratitude by simply practicing being grateful. Earlier, we said that gratitude was more than just saying thanks. We said gratitude consists of two components. Number one, it's an affirmation of something of value, something that is good, and secondly, it is given to you. With practice, we can train ourselves to live a life of gratitude.

"Start each day with a positive thought and a grateful heart."
– Roy T. Bennett

PRACTICING GRATITUDE

There are so many ways you can start practicing gratitude. You can show gratitude to others, yourself, to a higher power, or to "the universe" itself. I have used quite a few different practices myself. The following gratitude exercises and activities are the most well-known and proven ways to practice and enhance your gratitude.

KEEP A GRATITUDE JOURNAL

Writing down 3 to 5 things you are grateful for is one of the simplest and most popular ways of practicing gratitude. By regularly writing down things you are grateful for, you keep yourself in a highly grateful state. You could do this first thing in the morning, at your lunch break, or right before you go to bed. Some people like to practice journaling first thing in the morning because they feel it allows them to start their day with a positive attitude of appreciation and be more open to things to be grateful for. Others like to journal right before bed, and they report having a longer, more peaceful night of rest. By using your gratitude journal, the hope is to get in the habit of constantly noticing things you can be grateful for. You want to notice the good in your life, even if they are small and seem relatively insignificant. Although journaling is a practice you may say you should do or need to do instead, you want it to be something you want to do. So, if the thought of writing in a gratitude journal every day seems like too much for you, write in it every few days or once a week. Simply try to make it a habit. It becomes easier to constantly be grateful the more you get into a habit of being grateful.

KEEP A GRATITUDE JAR

This is one of my favorite ways to practice being grateful. If you have kids, this is a great activity to include them in on.
It only requires a few things; a jar or a box can also work; stickers, glitter, ribbons, or whatever art supplies you have lying

around. Decorate the jar however you like. You can use glue and glitter to make it sparkle, stickers, markers, or paint it. It is an expression of you. Every day, think of at least three things you are grateful for and write down what you are grateful for on little paper slips and fill the jar or box. Over time, you will find that you have a jar full of reasons to be thankful for and enjoy the life you are living. I love this practice because you can take a few notes out of the jar and read them to yourself when dark times come or you are ever feeling down and need a quick pick-me-up.

RECITE GRATITUDE AFFIRMATIONS

I love saying affirmations. I believe it is one of the best ways to reprogram your brain with the right thoughts and attitudes. Gratitude affirmations work in two ways. I like to look at myself in the mirror when I do my affirmations. You can affirm that you're grateful for things you have already received, or you can do affirmations for things you're going to receive. Some grateful affirmations might sound like this: I'm so grateful for all the blessings I've received this week, or I am grateful for the many blessings coming my way today, tomorrow, and every other day in the future.

GRATITUDE LETTER OR EMAIL

This is another of my favorite gratitude exercises, and some say it is the most powerful. Write a letter to a person you are grateful to have in your life. Be sure to express all the wonderful qualities about this person and how they have affected your life. This gratitude exercise's positive effects were researched and carried out by Kent State professor Steve Toepfer, associate professor in Human xDevelopment and Family Studies. In his 2007 study, his undergraduate students experienced enhanced levels of life satisfaction and happiness and decreased symptoms of depression. If you intentionally write letters to inspire people in your life, it will greatly increase your gratitude and happiness levels. If you feel down and maybe even depressed, you should most certainly give this practice a try.

CONSTANTLY SAY, "THANK YOU."

To practice gratefulness in our lives, we must get in the habit of *constantly* saying, "Thank you." Anytime you receive something good, no matter how small, make an effort to say "Thank you." This will help you to always be grateful. In addition to saying "Thank you" for everything you receive, get in the habit of writing "thank you" notes. Writing these notes gives you the time and space to actively think about why you're grateful.

If you concentrate on finding whatever is good in every situation, you will discover that your life will suddenly be filled with gratitude, a feeling that nurtures the soul.
~ **Rabbi Harold Kushner**

While being grateful doesn't necessarily make a bad situation good, it helps you come through the situation a stronger person than ever before. Gratefulness ensures that your best self always emerges from every situation.

There are few things more powerful than a life supercharged with gratefulness. You could almost say that gratefulness is like a superpower. Begin and end each day with a grateful heart and go through your day giving thanks for all the good things you have received and will receive. Gratitude will change your life in ways that you simply never could have imagined. These practices will lead you into a life of deeper, more profound gratefulness.

"The more you praise and celebrate your life, the more there is in life to celebrate."
~ **Oprah Winfrey**

Crown Yourself with GRATITUDE AFFIRMATIONS

I reflect on my experiences and past and give thanks

I am thankful for my friends and family every morning.

I start my day with gratitude

I begin each day with a feeling of love and thankfulness in my heart.

I am grateful for my work, home, neighborhood, and relationships.

I see each new day as a chance to say thank you to the universe.

Reflections

CONCLUSION

PUTTING IT ALL TOGETHER

Life can be a series of ups and downs. Learning to navigate difficult times helps you grow as a person. One of the most challenging times in my life was during the Real Estate crash in 2008. We went from a 7,000 square foot home to no home at all. For months, my kids and I traveled to and from different friends and family homes. I was in denial about what was really happening in my life. I was paying for a room here and there; however, I was displaced and in a homeless state.

One night when we were staying with a relative, my son asked me, "Can we just sleep in the car?" Those words hit hard. I could no longer pretend things were ok. I couldn't believe I was in this place. I was an engineer, a business-woman, college-educated, my kids were in private school, and I was still meeting with my Real Estate clients, but I was homeless. I remember hearing a message about letting go of ego, and I heard my mom's voice saying it's ok to take a step back, ask for help, and regroup. My mother had suggested that I go to a shelter and get some help until I could get back on my feet. It was a difficult decision to make; however, I had to do something.

I remember the day I went to the shelter. Just my daughter and I stayed there the first night. My son couldn't stay with us because he was more than 10 years old. They said he would need to stay in the men's shelter by himself.

I remember thinking there's absolutely no way I'm going to let my son stay in a shelter with grown men by himself. That night he stayed with a relative, and my baby girl and I shared a bunk bed in a room full of women and children. I just cried the whole night. I was determined to find another place to stay, or I was going to sleep in my car with my kids. The next day I set out calling shelters that would allow us all to be together. Some may call it luck, some call it favor, but I believe God made away. I called a shelter that had one space left because a family didn't show up.

My family was able to be together in a single room. It wasn't the

7,000 square foot home we had been living in; however, we were together. Every night was a family night for us. We loved each other in that little room, and we worked on our dreams and plans. The kids kept up their grades, and I kept working my business. Not once did I ever hear my kids complain about being in that shelter. We kept living life.

I remember putting together my first vision board and writing prayers of thank you in my journal. Most people that knew us didn't know we were living in a shelter. For about six months, we would get up about 6 am, do our chores, eat breakfast, then off we would go until it was time to check back in at night. I volunteered at my kids' school, so they had reduced their tuition. It also gave me a place to work on my business during the day. After school, the kids played sports, and we headed to the gym, the library, or the coffee house.

We went anyplace we could find free Wi-Fi so we could do our work. I cried many nights; however, there was never a hopeless night. I knew this situation would pass. We practiced saying positive affirmations and speaking about what we wanted our lives to look like. We even invited the other kids at the shelter to join us to visit environments that motivated us as often as possible.

One day one of the investors I had been working with came in town and invited the kids and me out for lunch. They asked me to check out a house they were thinking about purchasing. After I inspected the house for them, to my surprise, they said they had already bought the home for my family and me.

Going through that period of my life, I learned so much about myself and what truly makes me happy. I learned that staying positive helped me make it through those challenging times and helped me become a better person through the process. I remember being on an emotional roller coaster. I had to overcome my own limiting beliefs and those of the people around me. I focused on the things I could control and practiced good work ethics and habits in my business and with my children. As we practiced being grateful, the difficult times we experienced seem completely insignificant.

We've all gone through different struggles in our lives. Sometimes we lose ourselves in our problems and forget who we are. Sometimes we tell ourselves that the problem isn't there, or we find ourselves repeating the same mistakes over and over again.

We've talked about being your true authentic self, about being self-aware and self-accepting. We've talked about having the right mindset and removing limiting beliefs that have been holding you back. We've talked about setting good goals and even being grateful in every situation. Talking about those things is great; however, if you don't apply them to your life, you will continue to always get what you've always had. You may have heard the statement before, to have what you've never had, you have to do what you've never done. Change requires action. You can't go forward if you don't change something.

A small book shows the analogy between the journey of life and walking down the street. When I first heard this story, I immediately realized it could be the story of my life.

There's a Hole in My Sidewalk– by Portia Nelson

Chapter I

I walk down the street.
There is a deep hole in the sidewalk.
I fall in.
I am lost... I am hopeless.
It isn't my fault.
It takes forever to find a way out.

Chapter II

I walk down the same street.
There is a deep hole in the sidewalk.
I pretend I don't see it.
I fall in again.
I can't believe I am in this same place.
But it isn't my fault.
It still takes a long time to get out.

Chapter III

I walk down the same street.
There is a deep hole in the sidewalk.
I see it there.

I still fall in... it's a habit... but,
My eyes are open.
I know where I am.
It is my fault.
I get out immediately.

Chapter IV

I walk down the same street.
There is a deep hole in the sidewalk.
I walk around it.

Chapter V

I walk down another street.

Like the poem, I had fallen down a hole. At first, I was in denial. I blamed the market crash, my husband, and everything around me for my position in life. It wasn't until I finally realized I had to take responsibility for my life that things began to change in my life. If I was going to turn things around, I needed to get out of my own way. I had to step up and be the Queen that I was born to be.

Are you ready to be the Queen you were destined to be? Are you ready to design the life you desire? If you were to write your story, how would it go? I hope you are compelled to be yourself. We are constantly pulled in a direction to be like someone else. As we've discussed, when you embrace your authenticity and present yourself honestly, you'll no longer feel the need to change your words and actions to impress others. You can be you.

We have discussed living authentically and guides for solutions to incorporate authenticity into your life. As you continue to learn how to set your life priorities following what's important to you, identify and remove any limiting beliefs.
Remember to incorporate gratitude and new routines that will be building blocks to help you reach your goals. Discover the importance – and the joy – of showing the real you to the world. Learn to trust your own instincts. It is time for you to rise up to be your true self, be the queen you were destined to be.

Another quick story:
A father said to his daughter, "You have graduated with honors; here is a car I bought many years ago. It is pretty old now. But before I give it to you, take it to the used car lot downtown and tell them I want to sell it and see how much they offer you for it."

The daughter went to the used car lot, returned to her father, and said, "They offered me $1,000 because they said it looks pretty worn out."

The father said, now ", Take it to the pawnshop." The daughter went to the pawnshop, returned to her father, and said," The pawnshop offered only $100 because it is an old car."

The father asked his daughter to go to a car club now and show them the car. The daughter then took the car to the club, returned, and told her father," Some people in the club offered $100,000 for it because it's a Nissan Skyline R34; it's an iconic car and sought by many collectors."

Now the father said this to his daughter, "The right place values you the right way," If you are not valued, do not be angry, it means you are in the wrong place. Those who know your value are those who appreciate you......Never stay in a place where no one sees your worth.

Queen, you are beautiful. You are fearfully and wonderfully made, and you have treasure in you. Know your worth, and don't sell yourself short. Your journey to authenticity ends with a vision of your exciting future. Follow the steps to create goals based on your own desires. Make your bucket list. Design a plan that fulfills everything you've learned about yourself in every area of your life, from what type of home you want, to your career, relationships, intellectual pursuits, and more.

It has been a pleasure to guide you through these steps to Crowning Yourself and helping you to rule your Queendom! I wish you the absolute best as you move forward and experience the joys of living a better life.

> *"Do not wait for a coronation; the greatest emperors crown themselves."*
> — ***Robert Greene***

CROWN YOURSELF

REFERENCES

i Esther 1 MSG - This is the story of something that - Bible .... https://www.biblegateway.com/passage/?search=Esther+1&version=MSG

ii A Lesson From Esther, for Such a Time as This | CBN News. https://www1.cbn.com/cbnnews/cwn/2021/february/a-lesson-from-esther-for-such-a-time-as-this

iii Are you a Lion in the herd of Sheep – sakshichandraakar.com. https://sakshichandraakar.com/are-you-a-lion-in-the-herd-of-sheep/

iv Short Inspirational Stories About Being Yourself. https://www.inspirationalstories.eu/inspirational_stories/stories-about-being-yourself.php

v

vi Quote by Walter D. Wintle: "If you think you are beaten https://www.goodreads.com/quotes/1033193-if-you-think-you-are-beaten-you-are-if-you

vii The Elephant Rope. https://skillvisionindia.com/2021/01/11/the-elephant-rope/

viii CNN - Chatpage -Catherine Lanigan. http://www.cnn.com/chat/transcripts/2000/2/lanigan/

ix The Grateful Life. https://1w6y4jwic3y4cm53h2xzcm27-wpengine.netdna-ssl.com/wp-content/uploads/2020/The%20Grateful%20Life%20ebook1.pdf?_t=1591029257

x 13 Most Popular Gratitude Exercises & Activities [2019 Update]. https://positivepsychology.com/gratitude-exercises/

Made in the USA
Middletown, DE
18 March 2025